PEOPLE
OF THE STEEPLE

written by Ken Anderson

drawings by Noëlle

WORD BOOKS, Publisher
Waco, Texas

to
Marg

O for a thousand tongues to sing!
I love to tell the story.
All that I have to Thee I bring.
Sing Glory! Glory! Glory!

How quick we are in hymnal rhymes
To pledge our full devotion.
How slow we are at other times
To show the slightest notion.

A church by the side of the road
Had its own peculiar mode.
But mostly upending
Outsiders attending
Was how to decipher the code.

His sanctified image
Was left in the lurch,
When he broke the speed limit
Returning from church.

On-time Charlie is a man among men,
Faithful each Sunday like he's always been.
The church can count on Charlie's weekly feat
Of coming early for a good back seat.

I'd help you, Stranger, if I could.
I feel as though I really should.
But time is running rather late
And, to protect my real estate,
I've got to leave this neighborhood.

"If we are to build a new church,"
Said fund chairman Phineas Birch,
"We need help from J. Greenbacks McFudgit."
Phineas was to painfully find
J. G.'s nonnegotiable mind
Was such the church could not budget.

It's sadly ontological
That pursuits biological
And pleasures technological
Are more the kind
To whet man's mind
Than exploits theological.

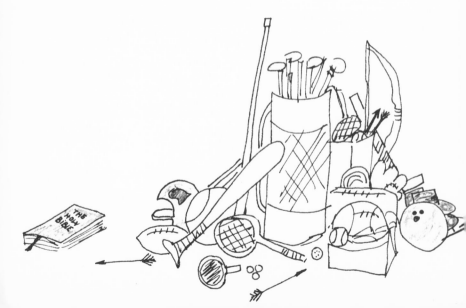

A pilgrim, unknown and unsung,
Was deeply and painfully stung
By a fellow-saint's gross ingratitude.

But though it was quite a deep sting,
The pilgrim could smile, in fact sing,
Since he had such a good "B"-attitude.

When Uncle Ernest could not sleep,
He tossed and turned and counted sheep,
He yawned and stretched, breathed long and deep
Times unnumbered.

Then one night he tried something new
He went to church, sat in his pew,
And, as he was accustomed to,
Promptly slumbered.

Chicken on Sunday can highlight the menu
Without being the meal's main feature.
While the pious partake of meat, then you
May find that they dote on roast preacher.

"Amen corner," decreed the proud,
"Henceforth shall not be aloud."

Richman saw what his hands had made
Of stone and steel and wheel and blade
All lavishly displayed.
But Richman was dismayed.
From the stuff and dreams of utopia
Emerged a fetid cornucopia!

Down at the station early in the morning,
See all the moneymakers standing in a row.
Which one has found success,
True inner happiness?
Eenie, meenie, minie, mo!

Consider the family named Trapp,
And the love they gave each little chap.
But think of the trauma
To miss out on the drama
Of the Generation Gap!

Hyper-piety, ersatz,
Tends to tie a saint in nots.

Our Father who art in heaven,
Hallowed be thy name,
And indolent be thy people—
Week after week the same!

Thank God for the economy—
Mercantile and agronomy!
Highways, airways, rockets in space,
Survival in the armament race,
Paychecks, benefits from the till,
Car and house and . . . tut, tut . . . the pil
Bountiful life in ample store.
Anything else to thank God for?

"Though I love my church,"
Said faithful Herman,
"Happiness is
A finished sermon."

According to the angel who
Inscribes the acts of men
(All the things we say and do)
With a celestial pen,

Gossip, malice, jealousy
(Spoken, thought, and heard)
Are in the category
Of a four-letter word.

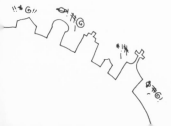

No urban squalor
More poverty brings
Than using people
And loving things.

See the Christians on a tour.
See their new things from the store.

See their baggage, traveler's checks,
Cameras hanging from their necks.

See how great is their emotion
As they fly across the ocean.

See them cast a pious eye
As the liquor cart goes by.

See how they all briefly pray
As they get a dinner tray.

See them visit many places,
Strange buildings, strange faces.

Tokyo and Singapore,
Beirut, Bangkok, Bangalore.

See the strange food make them nervous.
See them criticize the service.

See them taking photographs.
See the "Native" how he laughs.

See them buying many things,
Watches, trinkets, rugs, and rings.

See them at a mission station
Shocked at the accommodation.

See them quickly click and search
For things to show and tell at church.

See them rise at dawn's first light
So they do not miss their flight.

See the Christian tourists leave.
See the missionary grieve.

Hear him sigh, "What tragedy!
My brothers looked but did not see!"

Souls are dying? What a pity!
Quick! Let's name a new committee!

Said Dr. Tittle to Dr. Jot,
"We most assuredly cannot
Accept the views of Dr. Knox, he
Tends to be a little foxy
About his orthodoxy."

"Agreed!" said Dr. Jot to Tittle.
"His eschatology is brittle,
And I'm not very pleased at all
The way he views the Adamic fall
Or treats the Apostle Paul."

"And, speaking frankly," Tittle stammered,
"I am not the least enamored
By what I'm reading now and then
Of theological acumen
From your prolific pen."

"Ditto!" Dr. Jot exclaimed,
Appalled to have his views defamed.
"From your glass house you dare cast rocks?
Deceiver of the faithful flocks!
Your views are heterodox!"

"My greatest task," the parson said,
(To fail it is my direst dread.)
A goal I always strive to reach,
Is practicing the things I preach!"

"It seems to me," said Deacon Lee,
"The Bible was not sent
To us church folks so it could be
A cause for argument.

"Instead I think the sacred ink
Was writ that it might give
Instuctions, trusted and succinct,
On how to love and live."

Aspirations begotten on Sunday
Are too often forgotten on Monday.

She had taught since she was twenty,
And she now was sixty-three,
But she could not be retired.
She had seniority.

She did not command attention.
She had neither plan nor rule.
But it really did not matter
Since she taught in Sunday school.

"Since God is dead,"
The parson said,
"And we scorn the Apostle Paul,
I'm left no choice
But to lift my voice
In praise to *elan vital.*"

The message briefly said,
Scant hunger for the Bread.
A church thus refined
Might best be defined
As the quick and the dead.

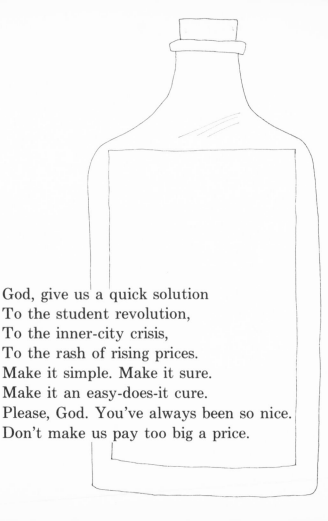

God, give us a quick solution
To the student revolution,
To the inner-city crisis,
To the rash of rising prices.
Make it simple. Make it sure.
Make it an easy-does-it cure.
Please, God. You've always been so nice.
Don't make us pay too big a price.

I looked up at the moon last night,
The deep, dark blue, star-studded bright,
And thought of man's race to the sky.
Rocket, booster, and satellite
Belching furious mortal might
Up high upon high upon high.

Then a new thought occurred to me.
"O God," I prayed, "if I were Thee,
How would man's exploits greet my eye?
As mighty thrusts, awesome to see?
Ah, no! They would more likely be
Fireworks on the fourth of July!"

If you read your Bible as ritual,
An act which is mostly habitual,
The results are prone to be neuter.
But if you read it in seeking to find
God's will and God's way, then your mind
Becomes a well-programed computer.

Savior like a shepherd lead us,
Give us ease and fatly feed us.
We are thine, do thou defend us.
In thy cause do not expend us.

Man's plight is rather clear,
Or so it seems to me.
It is his loss of fear
Of God and pregnancy.

Bessie Bagley loved the Beatitudes,
Though they rarely altered her attitudes.
So it seems rather clear
That the words she claimed dear
Were to her no more than mere platitudes.

To be fretful
On the terrestrial premises
Is to be forgetful
Of the celestial promises.

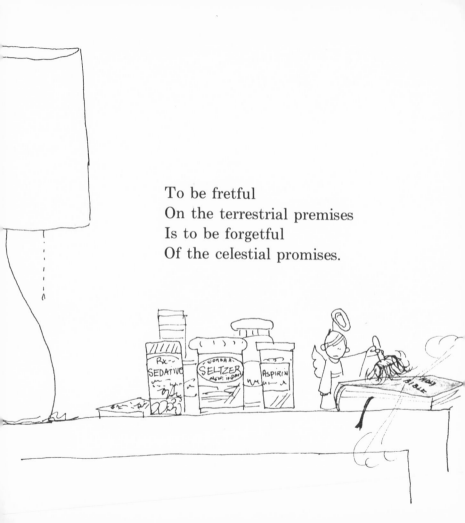

When you intercede,
It could be perchance, Sir,
The cause that you plead
Has you for its answer.

Factions and infractions,
Abstractions and protractions,
Test the fitness
Of my witness
Not by acts
But by reactions.

Annually each Easter Sunday
Socialite Clarice McBundy
Went to church. But this year
She failed to appear.
Her new clothes didn't either till Monday.

The board stood in need of multiple unction
To properly program its multiple function.
  Making the machinery go,
  Managing the weal and woe.
The Sunday school, the clubs, and scouts,
Bringing in the up and outs.
  Fees for pulpit dignitaries,
  Support for all three missionaries.
But they set the record for long endurance
The night they decided on building insurance.

One mark of the mini-faith Christian,
Whose Sunday is tailored to ease,
Is the mode of his spiritual feasting.
It's, "Make mine a side order, please."

Man is no different than he's ever been.
Check any era, dating way back when.
Society's the culprit, being more lenient,
And thus making sin so much more convenient.

The unknown rebel entered town
And quickly came to ill renown.
Wined and dined with politicos.
Broke more mores than anyone knows.
He left the "in" crowd in the lurch,
Wreacked havoc for the local church,
But carved a niche in history,
This "rabbler" from Galilee!

Bill was christened at the church,
And later therein married.
Years passed, and he returned once more,
This time to be buried.

Told to make the last rites brief,
The parson wisely scratched
A short obituary:
"Hatched, matched, and dispatched."